Smithsonian

LITTLE EXPLORER

DOGS

by Martha E. H. Rustad

CAPSTONE PRESS
a capstone imprint

Little Explorer is published by Capstone Press,
1710 Roe Crest Drive, North Mankato, Minnesota 56003
www.capstonepub.com

Library of Congress Cataloging-in-Publication Data
Rustad, Martha E. H. (Martha Elizabeth Hillman), 1975–
Dogs / by Martha E. H. Rustad.
pages cm. — (Smithsonian little explorer. Little scientist)
Summary: "Simple text and colorful images introduce young
readers to information about dogs"— Provided by publisher.
Audience: Ages 4-7.
Audience: K to grade 3.
Includes index.
ISBN 978-1-4914-0791-2 (library binding)
ISBN 978-1-4914-0795-0 (paperback)
ISBN 978-1-4914-0793-6 (paper over board)
ISBN 978-1-4914-0797-4 (eBook PDF)
1. Dogs—Juvenile literature. 2. Dog breeds—Juvenile literature. 3.
Working dogs—Juvenile literature. I. Title.
SF426.5.R87 2015
636.7—dc23
2014000186

Editorial Credits
Michelle Hasselius, editor; Sarah Bennett, designer; Kelly Garvin,
media researcher; Tori Abraham, production specialist

Our very special thanks to Don E. Wilson, PhD, Curator Emeritus
of the Department of Vertebrate Zoology at Smithsonian's
National Museum of Natural History, for his curatorial review.
Capstone would also like to thank Kealy Wilson, Smithsonian
Institution Product Development Manager, and the following
at Smithsonian Enterprises: Ellen Nanney, Licensing Manager;
Brigid Ferraro, Vice President, Education and Consumer
Products; Carol LeBlanc, Senior Vice President, Education and
Consumer Products.

Image Credits
Corbis/AP, 22 (top); Dreamstime: Alexander Raths, 27 (top),
Jagodka, 5 (bottom), John Roman, 8 (top), Mary Katherine
Wynn, 11 (bottom), Monika Ondrusova, 10 (top), Russ Ensley, 25,
Sunheyy, 14, West7megan, 11 (top); Newscom/Andrew Gombert,
19 (right), IP3 Press/MaxPPP, 23 (top), Element Films/Album, 23
(bottom); Shutterstock: Andraz Cerar, 24 (top), Anneka, 28 (top),
Annette Shaff, 20 (left), Antonio Gravante, 27 (middle), Artem
Kursin, 21 (top), BaileyOne, 29 (top), Castka, 24 (bottom), Close
Encounters Photography, 12 (bottom), cynoclub, 7 (top left), Dora
Zett, 28-29 (bottom), Emiliallngur, 13 (top), Eric Isselee, 13 (bottom
left), 21 (bottom), Fedor Selivanov 16 (top), fotostory, 8 (bottom),
Golden Pixels LLC, 13 (bottom right), Holly Kuchera, 5 (middle),
Ian Rentoul, 5 (top), Igor Normann, 10, iofoto, 9 (bottom), Javier
Brosch, 4 Liliya Kulianionak, 3, Linn Currie, 7, Margo Harrison,
24 (middle), Matt Hayward, 12 (top), Mastak A, (bone, paw print
art), ntnt, (dog silhouette art), Pavel Hlystov, 18, Phase4Studios,
30, photo2life, 32, Pukhov Konstantin, 16 (bottom), Rainer
Lesniewski, 22 (bottom), Raywoo, 19 (left), siamionau pavel,
26, siloto, 15, Smit, 10 (bottom), Stanislav Duben, cover, Tom
Biegalski, 20 (right), violetblue, 27 (bottom), VKarlov, 17, yuris, 6
(top), Zuzule, 1; Superstock: Belinda Images, 9 (top), Kevin Oke/
All Canada Photos, 6 (bottom)

For Jay, Shane, Daisy, Prince, Rex, Spook, and Freya. —MEHR

Printed in the United States of America in Stevens Point, Wisconsin.
032014   008092WZF14

TABLE OF CONTENTS

HISTORY OF DOGS

A friendly lick. A woof hello. A wagging tail.

A dog is so happy to see its owners when they get home.

Dogs and people have lived together for thousands of years.

The first pet dogs helped people hunt.

Today dogs are friends and helpers.

Foxes, wolves, and dogs are all in the same animal family.

The first pet dogs lived 33,000 years ago.

In ancient Egypt it was common for a king or queen's favorite dog to be buried with the ruler.

pharaoh hound

5

DOG JOBS

Dogs help people by doing many different jobs.

Farm dogs herd animals. They run fast around sheep, cows, or goats. Barks and nips tell the animals where to go.

Herding dogs keep animals away from danger.

Some dog breeds have a strong herding instinct. If they don't have animals to herd, they will herd their owners' kids!

Hunting dogs help hunters. They track and find birds and other animals.

Police dogs keep people safe. They smell for bombs and drugs.

Search and rescue dogs find lost or trapped people. They use their noses to follow people's scents.

Guide dogs help people who are blind. They look for safe places to walk.

Therapy dogs visit hospitals and nursing homes.
People sometimes feel better after petting a dog.

DOGS' OUTSTANDING SENSES

Dogs say hello by smelling each other.

Dogs pant to cool off.

Smelling, hearing, and touching are strong dog senses.

A dog learns a lot from its nose. Dogs gather smells from the air and the ground.

Their sense of smell is about 10,000 times better than ours.

Dogs hear better than people do. Their ears sense high sounds.

Dogs move their ears to tell where a sound comes from.

Seeing and tasting are two weak dog senses. Colors look dull to dogs.

A dog's sense of touch is important too. Owners pet their dogs to show love.

Whiskers help dogs feel objects close to their faces.

FROM PUPPY TO ADULT

A litter of puppies squirms and squeals.

Newborn puppies cannot see or hear. They drink milk from their mothers.

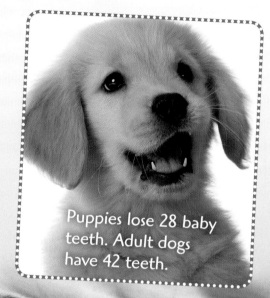

Puppies lose 28 baby teeth. Adult dogs have 42 teeth.

Puppies grow quickly. Puppies leave their litter when they are 6 to 8 weeks old.

Most dogs are fully grown by their first birthday.

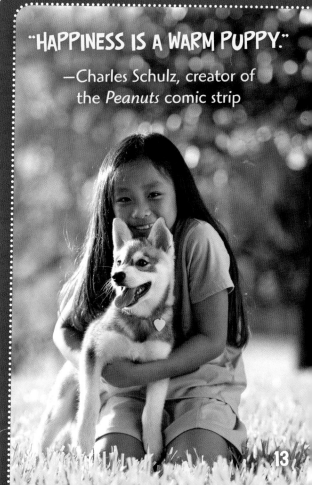

"HAPPINESS IS A WARM PUPPY."

—Charles Schulz, creator of the *Peanuts* comic strip

13

DOG BREEDS

A breed is a group of dogs that look and act alike. Each dog breed fits into a different group. These groups share common features.

SPORTING GROUP

Golden retrievers bring items back to their owners. Their light brown fur dries quickly after a swim.

These active dogs are friendly and loyal.

HOUND GROUP

Beagles sniff and follow trails. Their howls tell owners when they find animals.

WORKING GROUP 🐾🐾

Strong Saint Bernards can pull sleds over snow. Thick fur keeps them warm.

These gentle giants are friendly with children.

More than 400 breeds of dogs live around the world.

TERRIER GROUP 🐾🐾

Small Scottish terriers think they are big dogs.

They like to dig and play.

Scotties bark to alert owners of visitors.

HERDING GROUP

Collies herd sheep or even people. Collies are friendly and easy to train.

TOY GROUP

Playful pugs love to learn tricks.

Most pugs are patient with little kids.

Their short noses make them snore.

NON-SPORTING GROUP

Poodles can be small, medium, or large.

They like to swim. Their curly fur does not shed, so they need haircuts.

Each year, 2,500 dogs compete in the Westminster Kennel Club Dog Show in New York. For the first time in 2014, mixed breed dogs were allowed to compete in an event. Only one dog wins Best in Show.

CROSSBREED DOGS

Breeders sometimes mix two dog breeds.

Goldendoodles are a cross between golden retrievers and poodles. These dogs can have traits from both breeds.

Goldendoodles can have their fur cut short, like a poodle, or kept long.

FROM LITTLEST TO BIGGEST

BREED	WEIGHT
Chihuahua	6 pounds (2.7 kilograms)
Cavalier King Charles spaniel	18 pounds (8.2 kg)
beagle	25 pounds (11 kg)
golden retriever	75 pounds (34 kg)
mastiff	230 pounds (104 kg)

MIXED BREED DOGS

Mixed breed dogs can also be called mutts. Mutts come from several different breeds.

Most mutt owners don't know what breed their dog is, but mutts are often wonderful family pets.

FAMOUS DOGS

Balto

BALTO ★

In 1925 Balto led a sled dog team that brought medicine from Nenana to Nome, Alaska.

route of Iditarod race

Yukon R.
Nome
Norton Sound
Iditarod Trail
Nenana
railroad
ALASKA
Anchorage
Bering Sea
Seward
Gulf of Alaska

Each year part of the Iditarod race follows Balto's path.

SEAMAN ★

A black Newfoundland traveled on the Lewis and Clark expedition. This group explored the Missouri River from 1804 to 1806.

Explorers named a river Seaman's Creek after him.

FANG

A gigantic boarhound slobbers on Harry Potter in books and movies.

Fang belongs to Harry's friend Hagrid. Hagrid says Fang is not brave, but he is loyal.

Boarhound is another name for Great Dane.

LASSIE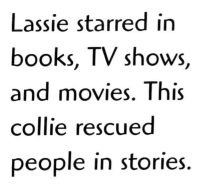

Lassie starred in books, TV shows, and movies. This collie rescued people in stories.

Many dogs played the character Lassie.

Lassie, 2005

DOG SPORTS

Some dogs play sports.

Owners train dogs for agility events. Dogs run up ramps and jump through hoops.

Disc dogs catch discs flying high in the air.

Some dogs jump off docks into water. People measure how far they jump.

In flyball, dogs race over hurdles and fetch a ball.

Owners train and reward these skilled dog athletes.

TRY THIS!

A dog named Taz once jumped 31 feet (9.4 meters)! Measure that distance with a measuring tape. Mark it with sidewalk chalk. How far can *you* jump?

A PET DOG

Pet dogs need a lot of care. They must have fresh water and food every day.

Daily walks and attention help keep dogs happy and healthy. Some dogs need brushing, haircuts, and nail trims.

Dogs even need shots! They should see a veterinarian every year.

Dogs use shampoo and toothpaste made just for them. Some dog toothpaste tastes like chicken!

A pet owner spends about $230 each year on vet care for a healthy pet. Owners of a medium-sized dog will spend about $250 on its food each year.

Pet owners must choose a dog carefully. Which dog will be a good match for their family and lifestyle?

Puppies are cute and fun. But training them takes a lot of time.

Many dogs live in shelters. They wait for a new owner to take them home.

Pet dogs are loyal and loving. A dog can be a friend for life.

Almost half of American homes have a pet dog.

GLOSSARY

agility—the ability to move quickly and easily

breed—a group of animals that look and act alike

expedition—a group that explores a new place

herd—to gather animals into a group

hunt—to find and catch animals for food

instinct—behavior that is natural rather than learned

litter—a group of animals born at one time to one female

pant—to breathe heavily

retrieve—to bring something back

sense—one of the main ways to learn about surroundings; seeing, hearing, touching, tasting, and smelling are the five senses

shed—to lose hair

shelter—a place that takes care of lost or stray animals

trait—to follow by smelling

track—something that makes an animal different from another

veterinarian—a doctor trained to take care of animals

CRITICAL THINKING USING THE COMMON CORE

Dogs can have jobs, such as herding animals or working as police dogs and therapy dogs. Describe a time when you've seen a dog working. (Integration of Knowledge and Ideas)

Look at the picture on page 25. What is the dog doing? Use the clues in the photo and the text to help you find the answer. (Key Ideas and Details)

Some dogs compete in agility sports. What does agility mean? What clues from the text help you with your answer? (Craft and Structure)

READ MORE

Ganeri, Anita. *Ruff's Guide to Caring for Your Dog.* Pets' Guides. Chicago: Capstone Heinemann Library, 2013.

Kawa, Katie. *Lovable Dogs.* Pet Corner. New York: Gareth Stevens Pub., 2012.

Lindeen, Mary. *It's a Dog's Life.* Wonder Readers. North Mankato, Minn.: Capstone Press, 2012.

INTERNET SITES

FactHound offers a safe, fun way to find Internet sites related to this book. All of the sites on FactHound have been researched by our staff.

Here's all you do:

Visit *www.facthound.com*

Type in this code: 9781491407912

 Check out projects, games and lots more at
www.capstonekids.com

INDEX